We've Seen the Same Horizon

ADVANCE PRAISE
(expanded)

"This representative anthology highlights the work of the Red Salon poets. Their unifying themes are drawn from the myth and spirit of the European Heroic Age, which they wield as a foil to critique the dreary banality of our own, far less inspiring times. With varying degrees of success, these poems are an attempt not just to 'see the same horizon,' but, in the best examples, to transcend it."

—Joshua Buckley, co-editor of *TYR: Myth-Culture-Tradition*

"This superb volume of Traditionalist poetry is by and for true aristocrats of the soul. Of the thirteen poets featured here, some will already be familiar to readers (e.g., Christina Finlayson Taylor, Juleigh Howard-Hobson, Eirik Westcoat), while others are new and exciting talents. Their styles differ, but they are united in celebrating Tradition, ancestry, and connection to tribe and homeland. They are united also in opposing the cosmopolitan rootlessness and decadence of the modern world."

—Collin Cleary, author of *Summoning the Gods* and *What is a Rune? and Other Essays*

"Poetry is practically a lost art. In this volume, it has been rediscovered. In ancient times poetry was used as a way of doing things with words. It was not just a form of 'self-expression' or 'bustin' out a rhyme' to entertain the folks. It was a way of making things happen, both within the poet and within those who heard the words of a poet. The poems found in these pages harken back to the ancient modalities of poetry and more frequently than not make things happen. Poems are worthy of study and multiple hearings as the meanings of the words reveal themselves in their inter-weavings. That is what I envision with the works found in this volume."

—Stephen Edred Flowers, Integral Runologist

"Poetry was once an exercise of manifesting one's soul in the material world through the medium of language and meter. Today, it has primarily been rendered a parlor game played by academics seeking to advance their careers, who, like children, have little contact with the world outside of their proverbial ivory towers. The poets in this volume, fortunately, are not among them. They are knights on a quest who have answered the forgotten calling of another age, listening to their blood instead of their contemporaries, and have brought back words of Truth inscribed on paper from their adventures – Truth which has been hewn out of the rocks of experience and the deepest love. Forget today, and listen to the songs of yesterday and tomorrow as you immerse yourself in these pages."

—John Morgan, editor at Counter-Currents Publishing

"Among many other things Odin is the god of poetry and this inspiring compendium of poetry and verse is testament to how strong and vibrant the Odinic revival has become in our time. It is poetry of strength, rebirth and consciousness that projects us toward the horizon that is our collective future and our individual attainment."

—Richard Rudgley, author of several books including *The Return of Odin: The Modern Renaissance of Pagan Imagination*

We've Seen the Same Horizon

Poems of Awakening
by the
Red Salon Poets

2019

We've Seen the Same Horizon:
Poems of Awakening by the Red Salon Poets
Copyright © 2019 The Red Salon

All rights reserved. The Red Salon is the copyright holder for the collective work, and the individual poets are the copyright owners of their own work herein. All poems used by permission.

ISBN 978-1-7335979-9-9

Edited by Christina Finlayson Taylor

Red Salon monogram designed by Nicholas G. Tesluk

Other images used are in the public domain.

The Red Salon
PO Box 354
West Union, WV 26456

Contents

Editor's Preface	xi
Introduction by Robert N. Taylor	3
Rise and Reach the Gods! by Eirik Westcoat	7
Per Aspera Ad Astra by Juleigh Howard-Hobson	12
The Glory of Hyboria by Lennart Svensson	13
Debussy by Matthew Wildermuth	14
Awen by Jason O'Toole	15
Replanting by David Yorkshire	17
Donar's Oak by Carolyn Emerick	18
Sacred Grove by Albie A. Gogel	20
Golden Spring by Christina Finlayson Taylor	21
That of Which I Am by Troy Wisehart	22
Blóðugr by Juleigh Howard-Hobson	23
Blutachse / The Axis of Blood by Siegfried Manteuffel	24
I Am the Holy Flame by Lennart Svensson	28
The Corn Pop Queen by Jason O'Toole	29
The Fool by Amelia Beechwood	31

Progress
  by David Yorkshire   32

The Ruin
  by Matthew Wildermuth   33

Through the Thicket of Time
  by Albie A. Gogel   34

The Warrior's Journey
  by Carolyn Emerick   36

The Ash Leaves
  by Juleigh Howard-Hobson   38

Under the Weeping Willow
  by Jason O'Toole   39

In Deep Dreams
  by Amelia Beechwood   40

Oracle of Our Mind
  by Albie A. Gogel   41

Zauber / Magic
  by Siegfried Manteuffel   42

What Beauty Waits
  by Christina Finlayson Taylor   44

Sonnet to Freya
  by Juleigh Howard-Hobson   45

Palearctic Grandeur
  by Lennart Svensson   46

Fólksdrápa
  by Eirik Westcoat   47

The Raven's Speech
  by Albie A. Gogel   51

Ansuz
  by Jason O'Toole   53

The Sacred Quickening
  by Juleigh Howard-Hobson   55

Morgenröte / Morning's Red
  by Siegfried Manteuffel   56

A New Son Rises by David Yorkshire	58
Ultima by Juleigh Howard-Hobson	59
Allow Me to Introduce Myself by Amelia Beechwood	60
Son of Sweden by Lennart Svensson	63
Eye of the Maelström by David Yorkshire	65
Skald's Saga by Carolyn Emerick	66
Shine by Christina Finlayson Taylor	67
Aboard the Lincoln Trolley Along Heart River by Matthew Wildermuth	68
White Woods by Jason O'Toole	70
The Tasks of the Ages by Troy Wisehart	71
Mit Rosen, Mit Schwert / With Roses, With Sword by Siegfried Manteuffel	72
Hanging from a Tree by Eirik Westcoat	74
Alignment by Christina Finlayson Taylor	76
Fate's Tapestry by Albie A. Gogel	77
Moosleute by Juleigh Howard-Hobson	79
Die Achse / The Axis by Siegfried Manteuffel	80

In Defense of Animism by Amelia Beechwood	82
To You, My Goddess by Albie A. Gogel	83
An Earthly Crown by Stuart Sudekum	84
Applewood by Jason O'Toole	94
The Wise Elders by Christina Finlayson Taylor	96
Robin in the Oak (Wren in the Holly) by Juleigh Howard-Hobson	97
Vittra by Lennart Svensson	98
Belle et Bette by Amelia Beechwood	99
Ziegenbocklied / Goat Song by Siegfried Manteuffel	100
The Blood Gift by Carolyn Emerick	104
The Officer by David Yorkshire	105
Óðinsdrápa by Eirik Westcoat	107
Óðinn by Albie A. Gogel	113
Spiritual Superman by Lennart Svensson	115
And Now by Juleigh Howard-Hobson	117
Spring into Being by Jason O'Toole	118
Voyage Within by Amelia Beechwood	119

Lords of the Black Flame by Troy Wisehart	120
Out of Line by Jason O'Toole	121
Wotan's Plea by Carolyn Emerick	124
The Valkyria by Lennart Svensson	126
The Roots of Trees by Eirik Westcoat	127
Glorious by Juleigh Howard-Hobson	129
Argos by David Yorkshire	130
Sea of Stars by Amelia Beechwood	133
By the Shores of My Mothers by Albie A. Gogel	134
Homecoming by Jason O'Toole	135
Sumbel by Christina Finlayson Taylor	137
Stonehenge by Matthew Wildermuth	138
Nordic Sphinx by Lennart Svensson	139
Sonne by Juleigh Howard-Hobson	141
The Thunderer's Might by Albie A. Gogel	142
Calling the Tribe Homeward by Carolyn Emerick	144
Notes	145
Acknowledgments	147
Biographies	149

Preface

The birth of this collection is a result of "lucky occurrences filled with meaning."

My favorite literata (Juleigh Howard-Hobson) and I were conversing metaphorically about mountains and mountain ranges as people, about how it is our own mountain that we shape and climb. I was awe-stricken to later listen to an interview of Stuart Sudekum in which he was discussing the metaphor in the same way. I forwarded the interview to Juleigh. Her reply:

> "'We've seen the same horizon'...that ought to be the title of a collaborative collection. Or a study into the foundation of our new poetical movement."

Not one to ignore synchronicity or sound suggestions, here it is within your hands with contributions by some of the early Red Salon poets plus several new contributors: Amelia Beechwood, Carolyn Emerick, Albie A. Gogel, Juleigh Howard-Hobson, Siegfried Manteuffel, Jason O'Toole, Stuart Sudekum, Lennart Svensson, Eirik Westcoat, Matthew Wildermuth, Troy Wisehart, David Yorkshire and myself, for a total of thirteen.

Among the Folk herein are active idealists, visionaries, realists; and regardless of the unique angles from which the horizon is perceived, the collective response is strong, dutiful, and beautiful as this poetry movement expands its light from Norrland to Cascadia and beyond. We share words of hope and resilience in a time when it's empowering to simply remember who we are.

Furthermore, here we share many mutual symbols, key words. We were unaware to what extent our words would weave into the poems of each other, and twist around and go back, like loose strands of knotwork that cannot be touched but only felt. "It's time," said Lennart. "Now the hour to be reborn is here," said Juleigh. "Now our Folk do gather," said Carolyn. This is our spiritual cohesion manifesting, and there is only this *depth* of cohesion where there is truth.

> "The world will not be saved by blind intellectuals or jaded scholars. It will be saved by poets and fighters. Those who will have forged the 'magic sword' of which Ernst Jünger spoke. The spiritual sword that makes monsters and tyrants pale with fear."
> —Dominique Venner

My gratitude to Stuart for unwittingly forming a seed; to Eirik, to Jason and to Juleigh for their ideas and support; to Robert for his support and for penning a critical introduction; and to the poets for being true to their high purpose (with some of them having penned poems especially for this collection, no less). Our endless gratitude we offer up and in to the Allfather and his ever-flowing mead.

And to our readers: may these poems reach deeply into your soul and stir memories of Ice Age strength in your blood when you need it most.

—Christina Finlayson Taylor

We've Seen the Same Horizon

Introduction

It is with great pleasure that I introduce this fine collection of contemporary poetry. It is unique and one of a kind in nature. Our goal at The Red Salon was to bring together an anthology highlighting some of the brightest stars within the Traditionalist genre of poetry, and that has been accomplished here.

We were certainly gratified by the response we received from the invitations we selectively solicited. Within, you will discover a collection of poems similar in their concerns and spirit, yet each poet stands out in originality and style. Each has a distinctive signature to his/her work with forms running the gamut from free verse, lyric, and flow of consciousness to classic and skaldic.

Poetry in our time has fallen into a number of pitfalls. In the academic world we have "poets" being milled out from creative writing classes that presuppose that anyone can be a poet. The result is a drear, lifeless outpouring of prose in a poetic form. What cannot truly be taught is the matter of inspiration, soulfulness and vision. These are innate and inherent in only a few real poets—not the mass of students being shuffled through the courses of the educational system.

Another factor in our age is that poetry has degenerated into the thirty-second spot commercial and jingle. Nearly as bad is the top forty musical lyric: a brainless repetition of words guaranteed to fill and to preoccupy the empty heads of the masses with a goal of material profit and cultural leveling. In this manner, whatever need the human psyche has for poetry is fulfilled with surrogate trash, usually of a degenerate nature.

True poetry has its roots in the archaic past. It is a part of what once was an aristocratic and authentic art. Kings and queens and the aristocrats of the lineage, where they still exist, have at most become figureheads and parade marshals. Only the poets have remained of this order in their original mould. They are the true aristocrats remaining: *aristocrats of the soul*.

Just as much as poetry has been a keeper of the past, it has also been a portent to the future. Poets are still the antennas of the race, as Ezra Pound so succinctly phrased it. Due to their sensitive and perceptive nature, they seem best qualified to discern and glimpse the future. Poetry, among other things, has always been (at least in part) a matter of seership.

We, via the Red Salon publishing imprint, are laying the foundation of a new poetry movement which is founded in truth and Indo-European folkism and tradition. Because it is not rooted in the corrupt and unnatural modern world, it will stand without artificial props; it will hold together and grow organically.

The Red Salon provides a platform for our individual voices and our collective Voice. With each poet sustaining a note, together we form a powerful chord. In that, the music of words, and a symphony of poetry that rings true to the soul, stirring dormant seeds to life.

Every poet in this collection is self-realized, has structured his/her own mountain of Being, and views the world from its highest summits. We recognize the horizon that we take part in shaping with our hands and coloring with our perception. We recognize one another, our comrades against the modern world who remain true to their roots and firm in their foundation. We are not alone at the high altitude where the air is pristine and the land is scarcely trodden. We are a collective body of poets inspired to affect the world positively.

So here is a seed from which a great tree shall grow, archaically ancient and vitally new.

—Robert N. Taylor

Rise and Reach the Gods!
by Eirik Westcoat

O Heathen Folk
in hall and field,
don't grovel to our noble gods.
The Bonds give boons
to the better heathens
as worthiness follows worth.

Óðinn is angered
by acts that are base
and empty of honor and dignity.
Frigg withholds
her favors from bullies,
the craven who shirk all chivalry.

Týr will drop
the driest tears
for folk who refuse to sacrifice.
Thor will turn
his thunderous voice
on cowards who cannot stand.

Freyja has frowns
for the feckless rabble
who lack in love for themselves.
Freyr rejects
ungenerous folk
who need but never give.

O Heathen Folk
in hall and field,
thank our glorious gods,
yet be worthy, wise,
and well-renowned
when you stand and strive for our gods!

Honor Óðinn,
and offer yourself
for his goals and works in the world.
Proclaim and carve
for his cult the Runes;
be worthy of his mighty mead.

Both house and home
keep whole like Frigg,
that exemplar of domestic demeanor.
With keys on your belt,
take care in your duties
for the health of kith and kin.

Trust in Týr,
and seek true selflessness;
put community over your ego.
Remember his hand
and make your sacrifices;
be worthy of the boon of the binding.

Be brave and with heart,
like boldest Thor,
and fight your battles fiercely.

With your stone steady,
stalwart and firm,
you'll be worthy of the valknut's weal.

Be forceful like Freyja
with forthright words;
have zeal for your desires and dignity.
Lead yourself
and love as you will;
be proud and independent!

Follow Freyr,
and seek frith and harvest
in all the deeds you do.
Free your friends
from the fetters that bind;
bring joy and delight to ladies.

O Heathen Folk
in hall and field,
such standing is worthy work!
But offer more,
and by aiming higher,
rise and reach the gods!

Earn the Runes
as Óðinn did:
thrive in your thirst and hunger,
ride the Tree,
and then rise again,
waxed in runic wisdom!

Spin like Frigg,
spare not your zeal,
and learn the layers of wyrd!
With wool weave
some weal-filled bonds
to improve your family's future.

Transcend yourself,
as did unswerving Týr,
for the power that binds great bale.
With a self that's serene,
reach the center,
the pole that offers order.

Through strength be holy,
like strongest Thor
who shines with self-assurance.
Seek the secrets
of his sacred hammer
to give the gift of life.

Face the flames,
as Freyja did,
and seek a bright rebirth!
From Gullveig to Heið,
she gained in power;
transform and fulfill your wyrd!

Be giving at heart,
like gladsome Freyr,
to know the finest frith

which grows the crops
and grows the kindreds;
through gifting, gain aplenty.

O Heathen Folk
in hall and field,
rightly stand or rise,
for the Ragnarök
is really coming,
though far in the future it seems.

Whether you stand
and strive with work
or rise and reach the gods,
on that darkest day,
there are deeds awaiting
you and the best that you bring!

But the future aside,
there's a fight today,
so aid the Aesir now!
Pride you may take
for your place in it,
but only if you stand and strive,
or only if you rise and reach!

Per Aspera Ad Astra
by Juleigh Howard-Hobson

We rise. Perhaps imperceptibly. Still
We rise despite this world. It is not in
Us to languish like lesser people will,
We were not made for that. Anger wears thin,
Impatience grates, anxiety and its
Twin, regret, do nothing but make us lose
Sleep. Leave such things to the common masses
Festering in their hopelessness—they choose
To do nothing to improve their fate. We
Rise. Every one of *us,* no matter how
Long it takes, how hard the climb; if need be
We pass the torch, but we do not allow
It to fall away from who we are, and
Who we will be. We rise. And then we stand.

The Glory of Hyboria
by Lennart Svensson

In the glory of Hyboria
four rivers fell into the abyss of Hel,
the Inner Earth of eternal reality.

Hyboria is gone, Middle Earth is no more,
crumbling in the upheavals of Ragnarok—
gone with its rivers, lands and circumpolar abyss.

Hyboria is gone but the sons of Arya live on,
migrating from the sinking Midgard
to the Scandinavian lands,
there to thrive for generations
into our day and beyond.

Behold, it's a fine day.
Behold eyes of blue
mirroring the heavenly blue.

Hyboria is gone but Arya lives on.

Debussy
by Matthew Wildermuth

No more stay these sails, but swell them with abeyance
To such elusive gestures as the sea accords,
Surge after each recursive surge, abating
To flood upon each moment's wave the next;
Expectant—heaving perpetually.

As upon the forlorn shores of Cythera,
Where scattered in myrtle and sand lie
Tablets engraved of lovers, whose soft voices
Have whispered into the wind, never again
To be heard—near on the sand rise yet
An array of columns near ruin, table less
But for the repose of each nutant dawn;
So beyond the ebullient luster
Which sweeps about the coast only to sigh
And recede—there yet sustains and heaves
An intimate depth, unrestrained by vision,
Conceiving of each fertile present.

So it is not that hall of sapphire
Before our yielding eyes to confirm the breadth
We navigate toward the plunge of sun
To sea—but a hushed turn to then regard
The dissipating crests of our vessel's wake.

Awen
by Jason O'Toole

Rare spells allowed myself
To scramble onto the banks of that river
      In which like a salmon
I was always swimming
Upstream

Times when I could see creation
As my children might
The wonder they sensed in all
      That to my cagey eyes
Had degraded
To mundane tedium

In those years, my small ones
Encountered mind-blowing
Life-altering experiences
In the day's minutiae
Accepted their truth
And pushed ever onward

As for me, the smallest sliver
Of celestial knowledge
Left me dazed
A psychic wreck

Never seeking awen
Awen sought me

Though I pretended that the world
        Was just as flat
As we students of nature
Faithfully recorded
In our spiral notebooks

However, came at night
Rutting Cernunnos and fiery Brighid
Thor the helper and Tyr the bravest
Troubling my slumbers
        Imploring rebirth
Refusing to sleep
With my ancestors

No longer swimming against currents
I held fast to a submerged cairn
Hastily constructed
        To a forgotten god
Letting river waters rush by
I evoked to simply be

Replanting
by David Yorkshire

And when you knew and said you were with child,
We looked upon the acorn we had grown
And nurtured deep inside the plant pot's soil,
As rich and brown and fertile as your hair
When on that autumn day we wound our way
Around the woods and found that first oak seed
And hung it by its cap around your neck
With Freya's idol, and I took you there
Between the roots of that almighty tree
And sired a son, our son, our seedling grown
And nurtured deep inside your furling womb
And given birth to on one summer's eve.

Next morning when you had regained your strength,
We took the seedling to the open field,
The sky as deep and blue as our six eyes,
And while you held our baby boy, I dug,
As lilting winds sang forth the joyous day,
And with bare hands packed warm firm soil around
That pale frail-looking sprout and said a prayer
To Thor for strength, as is the custom now,
Now, as our great-grandchildren take their sons
And daughters to the place where Thor's wind blows
And red-faced children play their hide-and-seek
Round tree trunks where the great oak forest grows.

Donar's Oak
by Carolyn Emerick

O' Mighty Oak Tree, standing tall,
do not let our brothers fall.
Higher than the other trees,
provide us shelter with your leaves.

Mighty Oak Tree, standing strong,
it's for you we sing this song.
Venerated since days of yore
by the devotees of Thor.

In your groves the Folk did gather
to dwell upon the things that matter.
Kith and kin, clan and tribe,
to live with honor we do strive.

But now we face an epic threat;
none greater has been seen yet.
We need your strength and wisdom now.
Point the way, please show us how!

How to be like great men of old
who were not scattered from the fold.
Strong and tall, they stood to fight,
did not surrender to the night.

O' Mighty Oak, we've come to ask
for the courage to win this task.
Awaken the Folk who still do sleep.
The Northern Wolf must save the sheep.

Sacred Grove
by Albie A. Gogel

As the frozen dew of the heavens fell
upon that once mighty grove,
the Moon changed in its celestial parade,
month to month, year to year, centuries passed…
And Time fell like the drifts of snow
upon mountain and forests green…
Sands of eons flew through the Night of Ages,
groves shrank and men became sheep…
Yet nothing truly fades,
its essence, its amber, its energy,
that nobility of strength and mind…
Within our souls, within our cipher of Blood,
within the sound of Name,
within soil of Earth & beauty of Tree…
Our Sacred Grove of the Soul still remains…

Golden Spring
by Christina Finlayson Taylor

Our golden spring awakens deep within.
The sacred seed, the Tree that cannot die,
Collectively a forest full of kin
Where mountains hold us high, where dawn is nigh
With morning sun: her mirror-children shine.
Aligning sight, there smiles the inner eye,
Unveils aright: our nature is divine.

We *are* the light, illumined from within;
Roots ramified through giants' bones; and high
Above, our leaves collect the dew, and thin
Veins fill with absinthe-colored light; and by
A winded limb, we touch the gods—our own—
As by design we need no wings to fly.
Inherently complete, we've always known.

That of Which I Am
by Troy Wisehart

My voice I lift up until that of which I am
The holy power with which I am filled
Guides my steps unto my purpose
I am awake and have awakened others
And though I am the increase, the dust
The spirit in my blood through generations flows

Blóðugr
by Juleigh Howard-Hobson

We understand this stirring of the blood—
Where the past and future are aligned. One
Heartbeat, one pulse. An ancient throbbing thud
We understand. This stirring of the blood,
It runs through ages and our veins. A flood
Of former lives. The warmth of a black sun.
We understand this stirring of the blood
Where the past and future are aligned: one.

Blutachse[1]
by Siegfried Manteuffel

Das Gold so rot
Von Eisen so schwer
Überdauernd den Tod
Drängt von innen her

Die eine Achse
Aus der Quelle deiner Ahnen
Hin zu dir erwachse'
Deinen Weg zu bahnen

Spüre sein Kreisen
In dir und immer dein
Sein ewig-während Reisen
Überall in deinem Sein

Deines Schicksals Walter
Der deine Pfade führt
Deines Loses Halter
Geh', erfülle dein Wyrd!

Lebenswein
Aus deines Stammes Hut
In deinem Sein
Wie des neuen Morgens Glut

Der rote Lebenswein
Aus deines Stammes Macht

The Axis of Blood
by Siegfried Manteuffel

The gold so red
So heavy from iron
Outlasting death
Thrusting from inside

This one axis
From the fountain of your forebears
Groweth unto thee
To guide thy way

Feel its circling
Within you and forever yours
Its everlasting journeying
Overall in your being

The ruler of your fate
Which leads your paths
The holder of your lot
Go forth, fulfill your Wyrd!

Life's wine
From your tribe's keeping
Within your being
Like the new dawn's gleam

The red life's wine
From your tribe's might

Lohe in deinem Sein
Wie des neuen Morgens Pracht

Heiliges Blut
Dein höchstes Gut
Heiliges Blut
Deines Lebens Glut

May blaze up inside your being
Like the splendor of the new dawn

Holy blood
Your highest of goods
Holy blood
Your life's blaze

I Am the Holy Flame
by Lennart Svensson

I am the Holy Flame,
I am the Holy Fire...

I am the flash in the firepan,
fire and movement preaching man.

Burning all materialism to ashes.

I will burn it to ashes, then burn the ashes.

The Corn Pop Queen
by Jason O'Toole

How could we as children know
Why a clown leered dementedly
From our box of frosted wheat
Our toasted oats or puffed rice
Or crunchy sweetened corn pops
Fortifying us with iron
We little men of iron
Princes of the breakfast nook

At the last circuses there were clowns
But they neglected their godly function
Ringmasters no longer released
Foxes with tails aflame
To cleanse the crops
We who bless our fields with Bayer Requiem
Have no need for some goddess
Whose name we've forgotten
Though it's printed right on the box

No pregnant sow offered
To the Corn Pop Queen
Who has time for bacon
In morning's frenzied rush?
No bawdy crone to lift her skirt
A plate of pork
A gift of mirth

As mother frets for a daughter late returning
From the winter ball

This morning's grains are born in sterile labs
To some, a crime against the harvest
To others, feeding the multitude
And wasn't Frankenstein a kind of Christ?

We are told by officious narcissi
The final circus has left town
No more lions shall be tamed
Children will never believe
In a bear riding a bicycle
Let alone give praise
To the Corn Pop Queen

And you who know your folk
Peer deeply into time's lens
See a child, holy fool
Laughing in delight
Holding in his smooth palm
A wild seed and in its form
Grasp eternity and know
That his spirit is iron
And his gods endure

The Fool
by Amelia Beechwood

Today is the day!
Recall all you knew.

Journeys begin somewhere,
right now even,
when you are zero,
nameless as God.

Progress
by David Yorkshire

And I the great inventor, my son,
Warn thee not to fly near to the sun.

Fear not my father Dædalus,
For should I thy son Icarus
Fall into the briny depths of green,
From all the greatest poets unseen,
Shall build the very first submarine.

The Ruin
by Matthew Wildermuth

I leave no hope in wails nor vaunting cries;
How many generations glide away,
Squandering so their faith; often this tower
Has waited out more fervent pleas than yours,
And will glow yet over your sons and theirs;
Winter, and winter still, and then again;
Do you yet think this wondrous wall-stone crumbling,
Or these arch-gates toppling are yours to save?
The work of giants wastes away and Earth
Has the mighty makers in its hardened grasp.
Yet how could this land become as new if not
First reaped and wintered? So seek not a peace
In these disordered times—it will not accrue
To thee; and cry not of the glare of the sun,
Nor fear—for soon warblers appear in thickets
Lush to announce their ageless song: "Returned!
At last our spring has come; the bright sun burns!"

Through the Thicket of Time
by Albie A. Gogel

Through the thicket of Time I have leaped,
that robust buck of true Nobility seat...
From a forlorn Age when men were gods
and chieftains ruled by generosity and deed,
not by sheer tyranny or that decree of a bloodline of kings...
Through the Forest of the Souls I weaved Fate's mystery,
the Norns' Tapestry of Destiny's true decree...
From that Well of Urð I gained council from drink,
White of form & purity I became,
luminesce I radiated once more...
Within Mímisbrunnr I brought forth Memory's key,
upon Lærad's branches I dined divine,
as Eikþyrnir I was known...
From the falling dew of my Crown,
whence all rivers rise, bubble & multiply,
forty seven and more, laid the course of Njörðr road.
At Hvergelmir the Rivers of Life learned the path of their flow...
From the roots of that Ash I sprang forth once more,
from death to life, my path has always been known...
Stag of Seven Tines, mightiest of Ygg's kin,
in that Grove of Wisdom Trees, Honor is king,
for it reigns above and below...
With a Loom of Fate, Maidens of Mead bestowed,
gift of Immortality, to uncover, to unfold,
the Daughter of Night and the Seven Stars our guide,
a quest of the Sacred Grove...

To that red-gold of Eternity,
not even the frostbitten wind from that Eagle's wings
could extinguish its glow…
From that Stag of Seven Tines,
sacred dew-dripping antlers bestowed,
illumination of Mind, helblindi to the souls.

The Warrior's Journey
by Carolyn Emerick

Peering through the portal
into the other realms,
a wanderer seeking passage
must first don the helm.

A helm of fortitude and courage,
and aching thirst for the truth.
Then let go and place thy faith in
the sweet dark sayer of sooth.

With cold and steely gaze
she will look behind thine eyes.
Thy words are only edifice,
true character the soul belies.

If the wanderer is worthy,
she will cast the runes.
To whither thou art heading,
the journey beginneth soon.

While this *Wicce* may be cunning,
alone she doth not work.
She enters trance and calls upon
the Norns who weave thy *Wyrd*.

Past, present and future
are written on thy web.

Thy place in life is woven tight,
but soon that tide will ebb.

She handeth thee a gemstone
etched with the Helm of Awe.
"Hold this sigil betwixt thy brow
and thy foe shall turn to straw!"

A wanderer thou beganeth.
A warrior shalt thou become
when thy weaponry and spirit
shall merge and fight as one.

The Ash Leaves
By Juleigh Howard-Hobson

Brittle leaves, the color of old dirt, lay
scattered wherever the last gust left them
in the autumn grass. There are no scarlet
patches, no yellow and orange drifts—they
don't fall here, under the vast woods that hem
in our place. We understand this. Land gets
what it gets—our land got ash. A forest
of ash, everywhere you look: great huge trees
with limbs that hold the forest up and cut
across themselves, interwoven amongst
each other's branches. With outspread roots these
trees lay claim to all around them, all but
the sky…which they fill, every fall, with leaves
the color of the earth, at every breeze.

Under the Weeping Willow
by Jason O'Toole

Oftentimes, inchworms
Would tumble from the weeping willow
Onto our heads
Into our drinks

We would rescue them
Gently set them free on the lawn
Dropped from our fingers
On invisible threads

Grandfather didn't get to spend his last days
In the shade of the willow's low branches
Smoking his cigars at the cast iron table
Painted white

He died an American death
In an antiseptic cancer ward
On the third floor, a parking lot view
Head shaved, sliced open
Beyond the surgeon's skill

I know I will always find him
When I close my eyes
Cigar in hand
Under his weeping willow
In his inchworm empire

In Deep Dreams
by Amelia Beechwood

Seen through solitary eyes, landscape
nonetheless forms our aggregate soul
without cease.
The wind against your cheek
has sung and howled and raged
the stories of our birth to all ears before—
tales interlaced in myriad patterns, but forever woven
of the same flaxen-colored thread.
Spun from gold.

Arms may never fully encircle
the breadth of our own meaning.
But the same mouths of idle chatter might still taste
that which springs
from all departed.
Taking in, digesting,
long past and forever perception.
Absorbing the truths of ourselves.
Knitting spirit flesh onto
empyrian-marrowed bone.

In deep dreams you lay your hand on my heart.
You know its eternal beating as your own.

Oracle of Our Mind
by Albie A. Gogel

From mists of Time we sprang forth
and shall once again return...
With wisdom's Keys and smokeless Fire we were imbued...
Thick as glaciers of Ice are those countless layers
of our death, layers of our lives, layers of Time...
Long has been the passing of moons
since Odes first were chanted
upon that ancient strand
of Fire and Ice...
Whence first we saw that Shield of the Sun,
whence first we came from Sea of Death, from Sea of Life...
Into the smoke we peered, through Death and Life,
Thought and Memory gained...
From within that cave where Mystery and Destiny
first held council with the daring and brave...
Such knowledge an aspect of that which is divine,
for such power of mind, set stern thy gaze...
Peer deep within the "shadow side,"
for vast is wisdom stored within the hollow of the souls...
Remember what we hold inside
as we once again unlocked that sacred Power,
unlocked that Runa, unlocked that Mystery...
The most sacred gifts from the Oracle of Our Mind...

Zauber
by Siegfried Manteuffel

Das Leben ein Traum
So reich an Wirklichkeit
Ein Schimmer von Gold
Dem Herzen so hold
Ein Hauch von Ewigkeit
Weder Zeit noch Raum

Das Leben ein Traum
So reich an Wirklichkeit

Magic (Under the Spell)
by Siegfried Manteuffel

Life is a dream
So rich in reality
A shimmer of gold
So lovely to the heart
A hint of eternity
Neither time nor space

Life is a dream
So rich in reality

What Beauty Waits
by Christina Finlayson Taylor

What beauty waits as though it's knowingly
More glowingly than outwardly it seems,
What runic patterns pose from tree to tree,
What spirit-critters stare and speak in dreams;
What ravens wait in branches to bestow
Collective memory, collective thought;
And what directions breezes blow: we know
Each sign is meaning-full, a path we ought
Pursue until we've played it, 'til we find
Another synchronicity or sign
And sudden serendipity unwinds
An open road. Each moment hyper-real,
We let the tendrils taste the air; we feel
The fields of others, the ideal
Of rainbow colors when we peel
Away the layers of the lies.
What beauty we espy with open eyes!

Sonnet to Freya
by Juleigh Howard-Hobson

Tree branches lift in sudden gusts, leaves dance
In green arrangements along sturdy boughs—
Daylight and cloud combine as sun shafts lance
The hazy billowed sky. Nature allows
Bliss to run its course. Flowers shift and nod,
Birds glide, then land and sing, light plays upon
Foliage, feather and stem. No slipshod
World is this, Midgard, this phenomenon
Of place and time in which we find ourselves.
Delight belongs here rightfully, as does
Beauty, as does accord. Holiness dwells
Not in mortification but in those
Certain things that can bring happiness to
This plane we must exist upon...and do.

Palearctic Grandeur
by Lennart Svensson

There is power in this song.
There is power in this song.

I drank wisdom from Mimir's well.
I drank beauty from Hvergelmir's well.
I drank compassion from Urda's well.

I roamed Jotunheim and Vanaheim,
I searched Midgard and Svithiod the Great
for the Impossible Freedom, I read runes of
the future in Baldur's Breidablik.

I wake at night in the peace of 62 degrees north.
The moon speaks in silvery runes about the
coming grandeur of the Nordic regions,
the Palearctic zone and beyond.

See the moon rise over Nornaskog. See the sun
shine on the pine trunks in the evening,
turning them to gold, pure gold.
Justice, willpower and drive shaped
the Nordic lands back in the day
and will shape them in times to come.

There is power in this song.
There is power in this song.

Fólksdrápa
by Eirik Westcoat

Fimbultýr's bounty
I bring to the Folk
and honor also
Oðinn's nation.
His holy mead
helps our people
remember well
their mighty spirit.

Our Northern blood
is a noble blessing;
ancestral deeds
have set our doom.
Be it Germanic, Norse,
or mighty English,
through the Well of Wyrd
it works today.

They bore the Runes
and battled Rome;
they conquered lands
and combed the seas.
Through deeds and doings
of daring in the world,
their might and main
have made them famous.

Our ancient ancestors
are an awesome folk.
Our Folk endures
with fame undying.

The roots of our Folk
had run quite deep;
a vicious conversion
they survived intact.
The legacy of language
links us together
across the centuries
of cultural change.

In legend and lore,
their lives we remember
to inspire our spirits
and spur us to act.
Their values and virtues
of vital power
are the holy heritage
of heroes today.

Whether old or new,
ancient or modern:
Our Folk endures
with fame undying.

Our Folk today
has found its roots,

rightly raising
raven banners!
Our ancient gods
we honor again,
bringing their might
back to Midgard.

We learn the lore
and live with virtue;
we rist the Runes
and rown them anew.
We rebuild the bonds
that bind the Folk;
we make it whole
and healthy again.

Our efforts honor
the ancestors well!
Our Folk endures
with fame undying.

With care the Folk
secures its future
and builds a base
—a beacon of hope—
for its work to come
in a world of strife,
for the road ahead
is rough indeed.

Restoring culture
and strengthening kin
will gird our Folk
against its foes.
But act we must
and always struggle
to keep our heritage
secure and whole.

Remember well
this mead I've won
and savor the sweetness
in the sounds I've poured,
for the precious poetry
in potent words
can fortify the Folk
with Fimbultýr's might!

The Raven's Speech
by Albie A. Gogel

For those who seek The Raven's Speech,
those who seek the Galðrar of the Wise sent forth
upon that Song, that Ode chanted upon the Breath of Time...
One-Eyed God, Simpleton's Bane, shed your masks...
Be necessity worn for Wisdom's sake.
Reveal that which has been hidden,
bring forth Runa under Sunna's rays,
some called the Light of Sophia,
through Eye of One we gazed...
Share that draught of Memory,
which upon that Steed of Worlds you gained,
from Són and Boðn, Óðrerir let us drink...
Not for wanton luxuries or fleeting and petty fame...
Yet for the Drink of Memory,
that which gives Knowledge of SELF Divinity...
that which shatters & destroys the fetters of Tyranny,
The Mirage cast before our eyes...
That which stokes Weyland's Smithy
to temper relics forged by that eternal Flame...
I howl forth through Breath of Eternity,
intoned with that Key of Mastery...
Carved out of ether with staves
blooded from the Wanderer's gain,
with that which was hidden,
with that which is named,
with Mastery of the Ages...

With that which was found in the enclosure
of that dark Goddess...
With might of Will I Evoke thee...
With might of Will I Invoke thee...
With Eye of One I see through Life and Death...
With Eye of One I see through the passage Grave...
I call forth by name, by those few have known,
and even less sung your fame:
Wōdin, Draugadróttinn, Dorruðr, Fimbulþulr, Fjolnir, Gizurr,
Goði Hrafnblóts, Grímnir, Gunnblindi, Hangadróttinn,
Haptabeiðir, Haptasnytrir, Heimþinguðr, Hanga, Herjaföðr,
Hjaldrgoð, Hroptatýr, Ófnir, Rúnatýr, Sigrhofundr, Skollvaldr,
Yggr, Völundr Rómu...
I call forth through Worlds 9 and two more...
I call forth through Cosmos,
I call forth through Breath of Time,
I call with Breath of Divine...
Illuminate Ye Sons and Daughters of Minds...

Ansuz
by Jason O'Toole

His staff before him
Scarf flowing behind
He is on the move
He goes to bold ones

The daring
Whose blood song
And laughter
Are one half
Of that ancient riddle

One morning
Between lives
I found him at his workbench
Walking through his wall like a ghost
I asked
"Why do you look like my grandfather?"
He must have known
One of us was dreaming

Dutifully inscribing runes
Into an official-looking notebook
Without looking up
He answered enigmatically
"Why do you think?"

In that moment
Of recognition
He called me into being
A mortal
Like himself

In that moment
He forged a weapon
A sword of wyrd
A wand of words

The Sacred Quickening
by Juleigh Howard-Hobson

(Ingwaz Rune)

And now reddened branches on grey root stock.
And now pale green thrusts of life in bark, in
Dirt, in pots: above, beneath, beside. Stalks,
Buds, leaves, stems, each suddenly *becoming*.
The mud grit of cold ground, the barren yard,
The empty meadow, the brittle under-
Brush—all yield and change away. So Midgard
Wakes. Again the seasonal surrender
Of ice to fire: dark to light. The cycles
Turned, returned. And now mice dip and drink from
Warm puddles. And now birds gather beakfuls
Of just-sprouted seedlings. And now bees hum.
Kenaz woven back on itself, Gebo
Repeated. Life urges upward, forward, *go*.

Morgenröte (Sonnen-Pfad)
by Siegfried Manteuffel

Lächelt dir die Morgenröte
In das frohe Antlitz dein
Ob sie dir wohl den Himmel böte
Trägt dich, hebt dich in dein Sein

Waltest du im Schöpfungswillen
Deiner eignen Urnatur
Deine Sehnsucht nichts kann stillen
Grenzen sind dir Anfang nur

Wandelst du auf krummen Pfaden
Auf der Erd' hienieden
Dir sei, so nimmst du nimmer Schaden,
Der Weg zur Sonn' beschieden

Morning's Red (Sun Path)
by Siegfried Manteuffel

Morning's red smiles to you
Smiles into your bright face
That this dawn may offer you heaven
Carries you, raises you into your being

May you rule in your will of creation
Of your own primal nature
Your yearning can never be quenched
Limits are just a beginning for you

May you walk on crooked paths
All along down on this earth
For you, that you may never be harmed
The path to the sun be destined

A New Son Rises
by David Yorkshire

Now the depths of Hel are overturned
And the beasts of Loki dead
And the morning clouds roll red
With remembered embers battle forged
In a thunderstorm of steel
Whose reverberations echo still
Underneath the dawning glow that burns
Through a nursery window pane
Two cool blue eyes gazing pale
Like two new-forged spears through golden flames;
There the babe renews the dawn:
Baldur, beautiful, reborn!

Ultima
by Juleigh Howard-Hobson

We've seen this horizon,
This same one, time and time over.
The blood red morning, hemorrhaged across
A sky gone grey. A dawn ever
Beginning. Never gone.

There is no time here, night
Doesn't fall. There is no ending
To the rising of this day. Nothing lost
To darkness. Nothing left blending
Into shadow. Just light.

Allow Me to Introduce Myself
by Amelia Beechwood

Lord of the heavy-scented blossom
Isle of Linden
fierce as The Wolf
with the blood of my enemies running as a river.

Stooped I stood, yet unbroken
under the weight of a heavy book
I could not read
with stories not birthed of
my father's landscape.

I am fiery elves bringing the end.
And from the beginning icy giants
cosmic cow-licked from the rime.

I am men who have had the privilege
of working their lives away
to owe their souls to the company store.
Dying of mine floods, mine fires and collapses.
Suffocating on black coal lungs.

Builder of empires, am I.

Crusher of my own children
under chariot wheels to save them
from fates worse than death.

Before time
I am fathomless limestones
set on end
by sheer will.

I lay, barely a memory, forever
at the bottom of the sea
after crowding onto boats
to escape the tyranny of famine.
Or thank heavens arrive safely to The New World
to be a factory slave, worth less than a well-bred animal.
Worthless,
Worth nothing.

I am brave knights,
and just kings,
and a fierce queen who would cry freedom or death
for her daughters and all her people.

I have worked serving meat and liquor
under lights, soulless florescent
to traveling, groping salesmen
to feed my children.

Migrated I have, from field to field
to feed my children.

Gone out early in the morning to gather
chickweed, dandelion greens, blackberry tips, nettle
to feed my children.

I am the dense Beech grove, the tallest Oak.
The jagged cliff dropping to the vast churning water
under the countless stars
which also I am.

I have watched my brothers and sisters burn.
Ran fast to the hills
saving eternal the chants and spells
and songs and power of plants.

Crouching, silent, silent as hares,
my children and I,
as those who first claimed this land
circled with the sharp ears of coyotes.
The smallest's cries smothered to save the others.

Bobbing on the surf, from afar
I watch my grandchildren
with their strong legs and weak eyes
who sometimes forget to remember
from whom their black hair came.

I am the dreams that blew away on the Dust Bowl wind.

The uncle who would look into the black sun,
to see the faces of the gods
within himself...

And you are?

Son of Sweden
by Lennart Svensson

I live in the Swedish county of Angermanland, by the Bothnian Sea. I haven't always lived here; some 50 years ago I was born in the county of Lapland, situated inland and to the northwest of Angermanland.

Both Lapland and Angermanland are northern provinces. They are part of NORRLAND as we call it, a mythical part of Sweden just like Scotland of the British Isles or, say, Texas or some other rough-hewn part of the US.

I'm a Northlander. "En norrlänning," as we say. The following poem tells about my northern heritage.

My voyage began in the heart of Lapland
as a Son of Arya, son of log-floaters and farmers,
eyes blue as the blue sky above,
hair yellow as the fields of rye.

I listened to the myths, sang to the northern light,
praised my creator and began my journey.
I lived among the flowers and the trees,
I read about events past and present,
praising my Nordic heritage as a man of the Svea tribe.

This is my land, this is my people; this is
Norrland, part of Sweden. And Norrlanders

are part of the Svea tribe. The Swedes
have always affirmed their being,
always been proud of their heritage—

a small, striving, hardened people
currently under the thumb of The Powers
That Be—Swedes, a people hectored
and harassed, a people crying out for
Freedom—freedom from the irresponsible
punks ruling them, freedom from debauchery
and treason, freedom from indulgence and
idiocy. Freedom to be what they are:
Swedish, and proud of it.

Eye of the Maelström
by David Yorkshire

You must suppose me older than I am:
Above my belt of furrowed barren crags
And battlements like ramparts of the world
Was once a crown of copper coloured cloud
Now black and white made through eddies and
The fury of the winds that blow the fogs,
Thick frets and mists out of sight, out of mind,
Out of the violence of vast vortices
That start with increasing velocity
To whirl in the most dreadful cataracts
To haze, obscure the eyes again with seas
Of tall colliding waves that ebb and flow
At fall and uprise, at flux and reflux
A splash of paint hits canvas, is followed
By other floating fragments—shapes are formed,
So inky blue a hue, where blazing forth
From a circular rift of clear blue sky,
The lustrous moon is an artist's glistening eye:
"I am the vortex! I the vortex! I! I!"

Skald's Saga
by Carolyn Emerick

If tonight I closed my eyes
never to awake,
would my life have meaning?
Or be dotted with mistakes?

Who will really notice
when I am long gone?
Who will keep my memory?
Who will sing my song?

Have I made an impact
on anyone I've met?
When I'm dead and buried,
will everyone forget?

I want to see the world,
and I want it to see me.
I want to make a difference,
and I need to live freely.

If tonight I fell asleep
and did not awake tomorrow,
I want my world to mourn that day.
I want to feel its sorrow.

Shine
by Christina Finlayson Taylor

It's time we underline our purpose, live
Productively, extend our lanterns out
For those who strain to see. Herein we give
This light to others: torches passed about,
A thousand flames ablaze from every one.
We do our deeds with meaning once we know
The worth of One, the spinning inner Sun;
The Mead of Inspiration as it flows
In liquid whispers and we deep imbibe
The essence, then express it lucidly,
And fluidly as roaming rivers glide
Along their course to grow the open sea—
'Neath summits steep to oceans deep—
And sure to shine like undines there.
Secure to spare, no need to keep
What light we're e'er inclined to share.

Aboard the Lincoln Trolley Along Heart River
by Matthew Wildermuth

(To my children)

Secluded in the soft peace of the trolley,
There recurs to my heart this eidolon
Of you, emerged of the pliant dim remote
Of all remembrance of these first years—
Emanant and defined. Meandering
The prairie course, Heart River glistens
To your vision, through the age-relinquished
Covert—aflow.

      Look now upon my face.
What reiterations diffuse and so luster
About the tributary's laden glissade,
Where sylphids tour jete their nimble tread
To impress so brief in billowed tufts upon
The rivulet? What mislaid murmurs
Out of darkness pour to plunge you in their gulf,
And abruptly then subside from waking thought?

When I articulate at last in but
These impressioned glimmers, burdened
With such mystery and lapsed from all but you—
This do I welcome, for you now reveal
To me secured, able, remembering.

For this have I suffered the passage
Of all hardship, and wandered through abodes
Of care. Oh, a song of my true self
Could I sing, of the tossing of the snow
On winter nights, when, fettered by the cold,
I walked alone the streets of exile, hung
About by icicles, bereft of friends,
With but my books and the bound voice within me—
Yet unproved. Those who know not of the roaring
Winter and icy wave of winds, who've pleasured
Not in the swan's song, who've sought not the journey
To strive their spirit forth alone, they cannot
Know of the longing in my heart those nights—
Those solitary nights of my yet-stirring voice.

As groves for you take on their blossoms;
As cities grow wondrous; as all the world
Seems new; as eagerly your spirit urges
Forth with the awe and heart for travel
Upon this lonely course, remember—
That I have welcomed this same suffering,
And I have welcomed it that this voice may
Reiterate at last through you.

White Woods
by Jason O'Toole

Like shadows on the face of the moon
Rabbit tracks in the snow

Naked branches twist like snakes
Or reach out straight from trunks
A selection of wands not for sale
Nor for parlor tricks

Why be eager for winter's end?
I'm finally getting acclimated
Don't even bother zipping up my jacket
Cold air soothing as it fills my lungs

After all, I will never see as many
Winters as I've already lived through
Each could be my last
Of course, that was always true
Particularly when I was young
Skating on ponds
Skiing trails alone
Joyriding on black ice

Like shadows on the face of the moon
My tracks in the snow
Pursuing aloneness
In silent white woods

The Tasks of the Ages
by Troy Wisehart

If one image only I could take
When to the next world I fare, this it would be
The ocean to the horizon within your eyes
With your last dying breath, you promised me
That you would be there to meet me on the other side
Now here I wait with the memory
Of the vision of your eyes looking up into mine
A thousand, thousand times
Forever, always, and without end we are this
I have been and will be thine, you are mine
We have always been and forever are lovers...
The green meadow, stars in the sky
Our limbs entwined in an endless embrace
I looked into your eyes as you crossed over
And went to take your place
I saw recognition on your face as you smiled
At the sight of familiar faces you had never met
You started to speak, then waves crashed
Your eyes sparkled, then went dull and you were gone
Now one last time I exhale as promise is kept
You take my hand and kiss my lips
The tasks of the ages we two shall now continue...

Mit Rosen, Mit Schwert
(Rosenlied II)
by Siegfried Manteuffel

Den Deinen bringe die Rosen
Dem Gegner entbiete das Schwert
Dem Liebsten sei Wonne und Kosen
Dem Feind' die Faust eisenbewehrt

Die Deinen, die sollst du beschützen
Dem Feinde sei Stachel im Fleische
Die schirme, die gütig dir nützen
Den Gegner dein Dorne erheische

Die Ros' dir zur Freude gereiche
Ihr Stachel dem Übel zum Trutze
Das Schwert hart du führe zum Streiche
Das Eisen dem Wohle zum Schutze

Mit Rosen zur Liebe gedeihen
Mit Schwerte das Unheil zu zwingen
Mit Rosen die Schönheit zu weihen
Mit Schwerte die Ordnung zu bringen

With Roses, With Sword

(Rose Song II)
by Siegfried Manteuffel

To those of yours, you shall bring roses
To your enemies, you shall wield the sword
To your loved one, you shall be delight and cajoling
To your foe, you shall be an iron fist

These of yours, you shall protect
To the enemy, you shall be a sting in the flesh
Those who kindly serve you, you shall shelter
Your adversary, your thorns shall smite

The rose shall serve you to joy
Its thorns to defend against evil
The sword you shall strike ruthlessly
The iron to protect well-being

With roses to prosper for love
With sword to constrain harm
With roses to consecrate beauty
With sword to bring about order

Hanging from a Tree
by Eirik Westcoat

That's how he did it, by hanging from a tree,
how Óðinn won the ancient runes.
He challenges us to change our lives
by seeking those mysteries. And so we must,
by hanging also on a hallowed tree.
But what is Yggdrasil, and where might it be,
that we may ride that rood for its runic treasures?
Everywhere, throughout and in all of the world,
the trunk, the roots, and the towering branches
of that runic tree are running, everywhere.
But gods we are not, so go for a tree
that's a tiny part of the total whole.
For each who has eyes, they're all around:
literal and figurative, both large and small.
Person by person, those pines will vary,
so seek a tree for your singular truth.
A regular tree at the Ramblewood site
isn't often special, but the Spirit emerged
when, with hooks in my back that harrowing night,
an ordinary tree was Yggdrasil for me,
stretching my skin and stretching my mind.
With time enough, I obtained the runes,
through toil after. Toil? Yes, indeed,
for work we must, for that wondrous gain.
For a limited being, laying infinity

into the soul and body is a serious task
that is wholly analogous to another hanging.
If nights all nine were needed by Óðinn,
then longer, surely, for a living man,
is the work of winning that wondrous gain!

Alignment
by Christina Finlayson Taylor

A Golden Age unfolds within when parts
Among the whole align, sustaining there
Within the Now. Apply the highest art
To all you touch, impart your will with care,
And lead relents to gold. This wondrous way
Of magic realism, alchemy…
This way we weave, we designate our fate,
Lets inner peace prevail triumphantly
When flaming phoenix-like we rise untouched
Amid the ash and elm, invincible
As Baldur (minus mistletoe); and such
That none will ever—*ever!*—break the soul,
The spark, the architect of *all we are.*
We court the gods, we serenade the stars.

Fate's Tapestry
by Albie A. Gogel

As Strands of Creation, guided by hand, gift of the Ages,
    manifested through Time...
Weaver of Destiny, a Tapestry of Death, Tapestry of Life,
    the Ode of Time...
As our Fates we own, as our Fates we weave,
    a Cosmic Will tethered to Night...
Strand of Creation, Strand of Divinity, woven by Will,
    woven by Mind...
To seek immortal council, to seek Wisdom's keys,
        to seek divinity of SELF,
To drink from wells three in number,
    Wisdom's Waters Manifest,
        Most primal of elixirs, enfolder of Time...
Further forth I traveled, chthonic road sublime,
past kin of Garm,
    That linen-white maiden's embrace,
      my most treasured of prize,
        bestowal of Death, bestowal of Life...
Gates barred my way, never to touch;
        stay true to the path,
          but use EYES WIDE...
On the barriers along that misty road use not alloy's key...
Unleash the training, those preparations of Form and Mind...
    Scream forth Songs of Power,
      those which fetters unbind...

Hell-Binder they called me
when weary and shining I returned,
Helblindi manifest in my being,
soul's transformed Will manifest,
                      Fate-Weaver I became…
              That wind-shielded expander of Mind…

Moosleute
by Juleigh Howard-Hobson

Someone worked old magic in these trees. Spoke
Galdr in our ancient tongue. Drew back our
Spirit from the ground like strong sap rising
Into the hearts of birch, the souls of oak.
We were forsaken once but now the hour
To be reborn is here. Berkana. Ing.

Othala. Our time re-comes. Again. We
Feel the throb. Drumming. Bringing what must be

Into being. Quicker now and ever
Stronger, soon we emerge once more to take
On form. We have been shadows far too long,
Almost forgotten, almost denied. Blurred
To myth. Named devils. Our return will make
Old ways renewed again. And double strong.

Die Achse
by Siegfried Manteuffel

Weiß.
Das Licht.
Der Tag beginnt.
Ich bin das Leben.
Schöpfung.

Schwarz.
Die Dunkelheit.
Es wird Nacht.
Ich bin der Tod.
Zerstörung.

Rot.
Das Gleichgewicht.
Tag und Nacht.
Ich bin die Achse.
Eiwaz.

The Axis
by Siegfried Manteuffel

White.
The light.
The day breaks.
I am the life.
Creation.

Black.
The darkness.
The night falls.
I am the death.
Destruction.

Red.
The equilibrium.
Day and night.
I am the axis.
Eiwaz.

In Defense of Animism[2]
by Amelia Beechwood

In order to be fully realized
The Self
might be ground to dust,
then reformed with the breath of All.

Which is, of course, God.
Before
you knew him not,
all the while looking
for a human face.

Seeing Him not
realizing not:
To be made in His image meant
not Him looking as you.
But You, a golden strand, Divine.

To You, My Goddess
by Albie A. Gogel

To You, My Goddess,
In embodiment of flesh and forever divine,
Through Eternity's luminous threads,
    Our fates entwined,
Norns' blazoned gift from Well of Life and Memory's mind,
Upon that mightiest of steeds, Yggdrasil, we climbed,
    Immortal Illuminated Consciousness,
That which stirs the Wind and moves the Tides,
    That which was written in the Stars,
      Ancient from birth of Time,
    Through countless eons traveled,
    Our Chariot of the Midnight Sky,
From frozen darkness through caverns below,
    Sung our Oracle of the Night,
  Howling Serenade, Symphony of the Wolf,
    Once again fills the helm of our mind.
My heart drips the dew of Love, that Blood of my soul,
    Through countless cycles of Time,
      Cycles of Death, cycles of Life.

An Earthly Crown[3]
woven from flowers out of season
in celebration of the First Marriage
of the Prince of the other world
on his travels through this one
    by Stuart Sudekum

1

Since roses passed from season in this place,
a dimmer arch of red has taken hold.
A prayer at vespers sounds as clouds unfold,
and rusty hues reflect dawn's vanished face.

A youthful doctor hides chilled hands apace,
skilled fingers numb from walking on the wold.
Disquieted by thoughts as much as cold,
he shrugs against the wind and night's embrace.

This pilgrim wills his heart to be at peace.
Despite disgrace, he's had no other goal
besides to cure the sick, and that *gratis*.

The ill reject the secret of the soul.
Though royal balm could mean for them release,
eschewing thoughts of health has made pain dull.

2

Eschewing thoughts of health has made pain dull,
but they with bitten tongues shall feel the sting—

and those who keep arcana of a king
will one day be allowed to ope the scroll.

Our lonely walker stops his evening stroll
and welcomes she who rides the gloaming's wing.
He breathes a word of blessing on his ring
to ward the night's uncertainty and dole.

Her orb gives off a wan and sallow light
and myst'ry broods atop a wooded knoll.
The shadows stretch: she swiftly mounts the height.

Each tree becomes an ancient temple pole.
There is a hidden place beyond all sight—
enclosure only silence may extol.

3
Enclosure only silence may extol,
she shimmers 'neath the pictures on her veil.
The truth is found where word and image fail,
eternity within the senses' lull.

Beyond the gate, a shaft as black as coal,
a cave beneath the fell that flanks the dale.
A fitting habitation for a snail—
the socket of a fallen titan's skull.

Though flowers of the field have passed away,
beneath the garden lies a wond'rous space.
The doctor now descends without delay

to seek for what the dim earth might encase.
A vale of bygone tillage in decay,
known to hold stones that prudent men enchase.

4
Known to hold stones that prudent men enchase,
this slope is sometimes combed o'er by the poor
in hopes of turning up some costly ore
by picking through the pebbles at its base.

Incised in letters time cannot efface,
an old inscription spans above the door:
a cryptic word of power used in war,
in mem'ry of the star that fathered Thrace.

The mendicants who come this far forbear
to venture past, lest one rock be displaced.
Exalted is the sun's fierce power there!

The master's scepter is his subject's brace.
With some, the crashing thunder is a prayer:
those men whose will no season can debase.

5
Those men whose will no season can debase
await the king's return and new-forged crown,
and following those things still handed down
show well the path the rightful sovereigns trace.

Strange symbols that the eons can't erase,
though writ in antique times of great renown,

still whisper on the walls of every town
though most will pass them by with heedless haste.

As ministers approach a sacred shrine
to light the incense in an offering bowl,
the young physician crosses toward the mine,

not letting fear or weakness take control.
En route, he spies a silver key: a sign!
Earned treasure in the pasture of a bull.

6
Earned treasure in the pasture of a bull,
found near the rotting wreckage of a barn.
The toppled boundary wall becomes a càrn,
memento mori visitors may mull.

In years gone by, this place was lush and full
and summer days were passed by spring and tarn
now lost but for the stray fragment or starn—
discarded trinkets vagrants come to cull.

Though fettered now beneath the coil and hiss
of universal ruin, life made null,
there is an adytum in the abyss

where every wounded person is made whole.
Though hearts and plans of men may go amiss,
monarchal eagles save what serpents stole.

7
"Monarchal eagles save what serpents stole!"
Thus cries his heart, surveying night's array.
Near Regulus, stars fall and burn away:
brief blazes passing while the heavens roll.

His gaze falls back unto the gloomy hole,
which leads to *imum coeli* 'neath the clay—
aphotic realm sequestered from the day,
the unlit bottom of creation's hull.

The moonlight on the threshold of the cave
reveals the work of some now vanished race—
a sphinx or dragon artfully engraved

with sculpted talons 'round a covered vase.
He knows it stands for that which he must save:
pure priestess who takes lions in the chase.

8
Pure priestess who takes lions in the chase,
the maiden who confers the hero's gift.
She sleeps under a veil that none may lift
until they have traversed the monster's pace.

This is the doctor's last chance to retrace
the steps by which he's come to this dread rift.
He trembles as the light through cloud does sift
on armored claws with scaly carapace.

He enters now to touch the marble drape
Whereon was etched by sculptor, long ago,
a carven sigil, sinuous in shape:

symbol of life, to some who such things know.
Nearby he spies a lamp with flint to scrape.
Enkindled, it gives off a ghostly glow.

9
Enkindled, it gives off a ghostly glow.
The statue's shadow lengthens and grows tall
and spectral figures dance along the wall:
deceptions that the fearful mind will sow.

As down into the cavern he does go,
descending through a dank and twisting hall,
he ponders how and why it should befall
that flint and lamp were here, the way to show.

Although his generation stays outside,
it seems upon reflection to be plain:
past wardens here were careful to provide

a means for him the way to ascertain.
He lifts the lantern left by unknown guide
revealing the interior domain.

10
Revealing the interior domain,
The doctor draws a breath in startled awe,

Beholding what his young eyes never saw:
bright lake inside a darkling subterrane.

Until he came, a stillness deep did reign,
but now on glassy surface without flaw
spread ripples with each breath that he does draw.
Light moves as stars upon the cosmic wain.

Within the perfect circle of the pool,
a central isle presides o'er this grotto
and, like the pole of all the world at Thule,

each breath of life exhaled must toward it blow.
It seemed to him it must be fate's own spool,
axis of all that seekers undergo.

11
Axis of all that seekers undergo,
the center from which everything must start.
The rectifying balance of the heart
prepares us for what wisdom will bestow.

The rusted twilight overwhelms with woe
the good plans that the sons of morning chart,
but craftsman's Fire may purge the coarser part—
a new Earth born beneath the heavens' bow.

With care he climbs down closer to the lake,
his aim a better vantage to attain,
by which he hopes to see what he can make

of what that central isle might contain.
He stops where Air makes minute waves to break,
now sunk into entrancement most arcane.

12
Now sunk into entrancement most arcane,
he stares into the Water at his feet
and sees what must be sorcerous deceit:
beneath, a boat is bound with silver chain.

If it were real and raised, he might obtain
a knowledge of that island more complete—
although this plan seems predoomed to defeat,
because a lock binds fast the shining skein.

Despair sets in, but he recalls the key!
Although he feels that it can scarce be so,
the chain and stuff from which it's made agree.

With such a craft he could the distance row.
On shining oars he'd span this sheltered sea,
cross over past the deathly Waters' flow.

13
Cross over past the deathly Waters' flow!
He wills it as he feels the cold depths' shock,
and diving, jams the key into the lock.
He grabs the chain, the vessel for to tow.

Success! The clasp is free, though he is slow
in pulling his drowned ship back into dock.
With lungs near burst, he drags it from the loch
and, gasping, sees the figurehead—a crow.

He stares into its drear and dripping eyes,
chest heaving in recov'ry from the pain.
Its wings are spread wide over where he lies.

The hulk exudes mortality and bane.
He empties it and climbs aboard his prize,
embarking to unite what once was twain.

14
Embarking to unite what once was twain,
he locks the oars and launches toward the isle.
He rows for what seems like a quarter mile.
His shoulders ache from icy damp and strain.

On looking up, he fears he strives in vain:
although he has been working all the while,
it seems there is no ending to this trial.
His boat is lost upon an endless main.

But harder still he drives against the flood,
accepting endless toil with stoic grace
and lo, his sweat falls down as drops of blood.

The Ice with burning Fire does enlace.
Some Thorns have borne unseasonable buds
since roses passed from season in this place.

MASTER

Since roses passed from season in this place,
eschewing thoughts of health has made pain dull.
Enclosure only silence may extol,
known to hold stones that prudent men enchase.

Those men whose will no season can debase
earned treasure in the pasture of a bull.
Monarchal eagles save what serpents stole:
pure priestess who takes lions in the chase.

Enkindled, it gives off a ghostly glow,
revealing the interior domain.
Axis of all that seekers undergo,

now sunk into entrancement most arcane.
Cross over past the deathly Waters' flow,
embarking to unite what once was twain.

Applewood
by Jason O'Toole

Lightning bolt sheared the top
From my wild apple tree
Crashing into the yard
Crushing a rose bush
And spring's first crocus buds
Barely peeking
From red clay

Setting out to clear this debris
       Axe in hand
Stepping into fairytale role
First swing into half rotten trunk
Sent scurrying battalion of cockroaches
       Second strike
Cracked the tree to her center
Blade stopping just short of striking
       A brown mouse!
Hiding in her hollow

Sweet Applewood, fragrant fire
One branch spared from burn pile
       Impatient, I began to saw
Twenty-four disks desired
Dull saw biting
Ragged chunks
Into the wood

My labor interrupted by none other
Than a solitary raven
Groaning in answer to each noisy pass
    Dull saw, overbite
Bit over-the-top, sending a raven
Just like the old man though
And me, using the wrong instrument
For the first notes of this symphony
    What did I expect?

The task done proper
Each disk holds snug
Her own rune
Divine names sung deeply
Into bloodened applewood
Sanded mirror-smooth

The Wise Elders[4]
by Christina Finlayson Taylor

Fehu brings me money.
Uruz: will to be.
Thurisaz, my weapon.
Ansuz: poetry!
Raidho, rod and compass.
Kenaz, a torch aflame.
Gebo, gifts reciprocal.
Wunjo, heights attained.

Hagalaz: destructive force.
Nauthiz is a need.
Isa says "be solid!"
Jera reaps from seed.
Eiwaz, yew and backbone.
Pertho, burst to flower.
Elhaz for protection.
Sowilo: will to power.

Tiwaz brings me justice.
Berkana, rune of mothers.
Ehwaz: flow together.
Mannaz: be kind to others.
Laguz, the way of water.
Inguz: incubate.
Othala, my birthright.
Dagaz, the bright of day.

Robin in the Oak (Wren in the Holly)
by Juleigh Howard-Hobson

    Sól er landa ljóme;
    lúti ek helgum dóme.

The world will not remain this dark cold grey.
Winter loses every year, therefore it
Will again. Ice breaks, need-fires gutter, hail
Stops falling. The axis swivels, away,
As it has before. Cycles ever commit
Their rounds. Frost that flourishes last will fail.
Everything changes. Spring is never late
And summer's not far behind it. A folk
Who celebrate a world ever regrown,
Reborn, is stronger for each frozen wait.
So light returns. Invincible. The Oak
King wins, the Holly King is overthrown.
Darkness leaves, followed by the world of men
Like warmth follows cold, robin follows wren.

Vittra
by Lennart Svensson

My grandmother told me about vittra,
shiny, silvery people roaming the Norrland woods.
They were not men. They were superhuman, they
were of elven kin, demigods ruling the land
along with the devas of vegetation.

My grandma left me a map and one day I will
venture out into the woods, follow the secret
path to Vittra Land, seek out the shiny people
and let them teach me the language of the plants
and the way to bliss beyond the Beyond.

And using a secret means to entrap one
I might find me a vittra maid and we'll go
walking over the moors and admire the moon
mirroring itself in a tarn, reciting poetry, and
dance to the rhythm of troll drums—

beyond the doldrums, in the lively
climes we'll skip the light fantastic,
"come on and join the elven's dance,
their wizardry and wild romance"—
the vittra leitmotif of eternal glory.

Belle et Bette
by Amelia Beechwood

I fancied myself Beauty,
innocent and fated
Queen of inner sight.

With this sight
I looked more deeply even,
into my own heart

To find, alas, I too was the Beast,
enchanted and unlovable.
But kinder for this knowledge,
and most importantly:
Wild.

Ziegenbocklied
by Siegfried Manteuffel

Gar lustig tanzt der Ziegenbock
So zagt er nimmer mehr
Und geht's auch über Stein und Stock
Er tanzt mal hin, mal her

Singt er frech dir auch vom Wein
Und bietet dir wohl feil
Er soll dein Lebensblut dir sein
als Schöpferkraft und Heil

Wohlan, es tobt der Ziegen-Herr
Er ringt und rast und reitet
Am Abgrund noch tut's ihm nicht schwer
Wie er ins Leben schreitet

Seine Hörner wohlgemut
Trägt er nicht nur zum Streite
Zeichen dir zu Glück und Gut
Auf dass es treu dich leite

Des Bockes Hörner
(Ziegenbocklied II)

Ziegenblut
Ist Ziegenmut
Und Ziegenwut

Goat Song
by Siegfried Manteuffel

Merrily dances the goat
Never he hesitates
And over rough and smooth
He dances to and fro

If he may sing of the wine
And offers it to you
It shall be your life's blood
Creative force and salvation

Well then, the goat lord raves
He wrestles and rages and rides
Even easy at the edge of the abyss
As he strides into life

His horns exuberant
He does not bear them just for strife
A sign for you toward luck and good fortune
That it may lead you well

The Horns of the Goat
(Goat Song II)

Goat blood
Is goat courage
And goat wrath

Lebensglut...

Zügellos
Reuelos
Ruhelos

Des Bockes Horn
Ist Lebensborn
Auserkor'n

Sein göttlich Funken
Nachtversunken
Lebenstrunken

Der Ziegen Tanz
Ein güld'ner Kranz
Von Urkraft ganz

Ein heiter Reigen
Das Blut soll steigen
Mach dir's zu eigen

Der Ziegen Sang
Dein Siegesklang
Dein Lebensgang

Capricorn
Des Bockes Horn
Dein Lebensborn

Life's glow...

Reinless
Reckless
Restless

The goat horn
Is the spring of life
The chosen

His divine spark
Sunken into the night
Drunken with life

The goat dance
A golden wreath
Made whole by primal force

A mirthful round dance
Blood shall rise up
Make it yours

The goat song
Your victory tone
Your life's course

Capricorn
The goat horn
Your well of life

The Blood Gift
by Carolyn Emerick

The air is crisp and cool,
and the moon is beaming bright
lighting up the clouds against
the velvet sky tonight.

And I feel alive with wonder,
and I feel alive with light.
For I feel the effervescence
that is alive this night.

For we tap into the source
of our ancestral might.
If we can read the energy,
then we receive the Sight.

When we see, then we can know
what is true and right.
Our ancestors infuse our blood,
emboldened for the fight.

And tonight I gaze upon
celestial white on blue.
I know that I am not alone,
for I'm in this fight with you.

The Officer
by David Yorkshire

Lain atop an ancient barrow,
My eyes obscured by leaves of yarrow,
Still dressed in khaki uniform,
Flecks of blood glow in the dawn.

As my life-force slips away
With the coming of the day
The present, past and future merge
In every pulse and heartbeat surge.

I see my self in other times;
Other people, other minds
Are but by speech and custom changed,
Superficially rearranged.

Revolver, sabre, gas mask gone,
Yet other battles to be won,
Wielding spear and shield and axe,
Leading bondsmen in attacks,

Defending hearth and folk and land,
Marauding with an iron hand:
Good and evil paradigm
Relative to folk and kin.

Now my time is drawing near,
As once the corpse upon the bier

Below the mound on which I lie,
Future visions pierce my eye:

My folk beleaguered, leaderless,
Ship adrift and rudderless;
No helm nor helmsman there to steer
Now the hurricane is here.

I see my people cowed and bent,
Prey to foul invaders sent
By foreign multinationals
Aided by our criminals.

Into this I'll be reborn
After death upon this morn
And lead my folk again when ripe:
Irrepressible archetype.

Óðinsdrápa
by Eirik Westcoat

For the master of mead
I make my praise
—that rowner and rister
of runic might—
and pour his drink
—that precious draught—
in the potent staves
of a powerful drápa.

Borr by Bestla
gave birth to him,
Búri and Bölþorn's
brightest descendant.
The etin Ymir
Óðinn then slew
and ordered the earth
by his own design.

The sun and moon
he set on courses;
each realm he gave
a rightful place.
The worlds were made,
yet he wanted more;
he sensed the unknown
and sought its mystery.

On the Tree he hung
with terrible hunger
nights numbered nine
in needful ordeal;
with a look and scream
he skillfully lifted
gainful knowledge
of the glorious Runes.

Joyous Óðinn
is a generous lord,
for among the worlds
those mysteries he shared.
He bids us follow
and benefit too,
by giving ourselves
and gaining ourselves.

He always seeks
to add to his wisdom,
for awesome Óðinn
is of Aesir best!

The art of Seið
he sought from his mistress;
of might and main,
it's a major source.
He laid with Freyja
and learned its secrets;
by knowing mystery,
magic is gained.

Famous Freyja's
fimbul magic
is another part
of needful questing;
through the depths of trance
in darkness and light,
singular secrets
are sought and found.

He presses onward;
no path is forbidden,
for awesome Óðinn
is of Aesir best!

Mímir gave Hœnir
mighty counsels,
until his head
was hewn from his neck.
But Sigtýr saved
that source of wisdom
by spreading on herbs
and uttering spells.

Of hidden things
the head of Mímir
speaks now to Óðinn,
adding to his knowledge.
The challenge to us,
if we choose to accept,
is to seek for ourselves
this source of knowing.

His many quests
are mighty examples,
*for Óðinn always
aims for glory!*

In the well he sought
transcendent wisdom;
but Mímir demanded
a mighty price—
Óðinn must offer
an eye to the well.
He paid in full
for that precious drink.

An eye for the tree,
an eye for the well;
in all the realms
he's able to see.
He never asks
of his Einherjar
for more than what
he's managed to do.

The powers he's gained
are great indeed,
*for Óðinn always
aims for glory!*

But the greatest treasure
he took from Gunnlöð—
the mightiest mead,

made from Kvasir.
Three draughts he got
for three nights' lust;
the sneaky serpent
then soared as eagle.

This best of bounties
he bears to the few
—skalds and scholars—
for skill with words.
To win and pour
that potion as well
is the mighty challenge
he makes to them.

At the end of all,
Óðinn faces
the giant jaws
of the jaundiced wolf.
He is swallowed whole,
and his son avenges,
ripping apart
the ravenous beast.

Transformed he lives
in famed survivors:
in Hœnir made whole
and as Höð and Baldur,
in valiant Víðarr
and Váli his brother;

a mysterious triumph
o'er tragedy and death.

His noble quests
I've named in verse
with this mead I made
and mixed with runes;
drink it deeply
and dare to follow
in mighty Óðinn's
mainful footsteps!

Óðinn
by Albie A. Gogel

Hail To The Speakers, Hail To The Hall,
Hail Thee, Ancestral Wisdom and Force of Will,
from the Goddesses and Gods of Old & Now…
'Tis it not I, Gungnir at side and upon Sleipnir, my steed?
For am I not the One-Eyed Wanderer of Many Names,
he who travels realms 9 above and below
on the quest for Wisdom, Knowledge, Thought and Memory?
All-Father, Tamer of Garm, Raven Lord,
via the Eagle of Blood I feast the Ravens upon flesh of foes.
Woden, and as Gangleri,
I am the highest council sought by kings.
As Sigge I was known, as victory reigned,
the giver of Draupnir's harvest, the giver of red-gold rings.
Mighty are the Runa I see, the Runa I seized.
As Har I was known
when the Pole Star cast my gaze from above and below,
to the well of Urd, that Cauldron of All,
I cast out my eye so I may glare deeper.
In battle's ecstasy as Wotan I reign.
With Gungnir and my steed,
the Lord of the Host,
Lord of the Hunt can never be beat.
I am Óðinn, sire of heroes,
sire of aspects of the divine,
patriarch of chieftains most noble,
and the true honor of kings.

I am the swirling winds of Madness,
the kinetic force of Will,
I am Destiny hurled upon the brow
and shoulders of the True, of Einherjar,
of the manifested Destiny of the Ages,
of the Tempest in the Trees,
I am thought manifest,
I am Har...

Spiritual Superman
by Lennart Svensson

I live in the mountains.
Far above human foolishness.
Teaching and preaching.
Declaring you the spiritual superman.

◆ ◆ ◆

I declare you the spiritual superman,
superomismo with a spiritual footing.
His name is Responsible Man.

Responsible Man uses willpower and Memento Mori in order to reach mental calm—C3, a state of "Calm, Cool and Collected." This is the way to be under the new, improved sun in the coming golden age.

Responsible Man goes with Movement as A State through the Metropolitan decadence, heading for the Antropolitan splendor.

Responsible Man embodies Action as Being, lives according to There Is Only Here and Now and performs Movement as A State, as such, a virtual wave of joy melting the glacier of nihilism.

◆ ◆ ◆

By way of will-thought,
I exercise supreme power over my being.

That's sovereignty, that's responsibility, that's freedom.

Willpower, zest and faith-in-action are the way ahead.

◆ ◆ ◆

It's time for the sunshine zeitgeist
to melt the glacier of nihilism.

It's time for alacrity and drive to sweep away
the negativist development in literature, film and the media.

It's time to stop worship of death.
Time to start worship of life and light.

And Now
by Juleigh Howard-Hobson

There is sun now where all the days before
We had only rain. Rain and cold weather,
And grey skies that never seemed to lift or
Move. A badly done still life that never
Was quite finished. Until suddenly, it
Was. And now the sun is back, the sky is
Blue, what few clouds there are, are white and lit
From behind by brilliance we reminisced
About just a week ago. It's here. Spring.
And with it the sun and all that sunlight
Supports: bees, voles, fawns, rabbits, yarrow, ring-
Necked doves, meadows of grasses, shiny-bright
Leftover puddles that reflect the sky
And sunlit clouds that springtime winds blow by.

Spring into Being
by Jason O'Toole

Heliotropic heads incline
Towards that majesty
Which sustains and gives
Their name
Whirling sphere feeds whirling disks
Flowers spiral within flowers
Beauteous symmetry, perfection
Angles irreducible illume
Magnificence of our great
Arithmetician

If we seek
That living light
Will she bequeath
Such golden life?
Enthroned in her ratio
Our scepters root
In yielding loam

Night-capped heads awaken
Beatific faces warmed
By deathless rays
Tilt towards eternity
Returning the joy
In our spirits
Enkindled

Voyage Within
by Amelia Beechwood

The cavernous within,
oh steadfast pilgrim!
Voyage the sacred sea;
journey to presently.

Through blackest wood arrive,
to your own in-most space.
Hollow noise replaced by
fathomless within peace.

Up, round and round again
this holy mountain.
Down and down, down again
within holy chasm.

Light withers, darkness blooms,
the deepest spark contains
it, within would-be seed;
divine attended need.

The cavernous within,
oh steadfast pilgrim!
Voyage this sacred sea;
journey to presently.

Lords of the Black Flame
by Troy Wisehart

I know four and twenty mighty Lords.
Their flaming crowns of black fire I wear upon my brow.
I know their numbers, I know their meanings,
I know their shapes, I know their names.
These burning crowns have been bestowed upon me
at great price and sacrifice of self unto myself.
Daily an offering I make of every crown
in return and contribution to the great work.
Daily I receive each one anew
even darker and greater than before.
In reverence and awe I sing their ancient names
in praise of these primordial kings
whose reign has ever been and is unto everlasting.

Out of Line
by Jason O'Toole

Has our language
Being linear
Caused our thinking
To be so confined
Over time, has our sense of time
Become as flat as this line?

Presented with signs
That vast nature
Will not be restrained
By thin lines of perception

Our ancestors surely abashed
To find us still standing in line
In the wrong line, at that
Arranging our work-life
And leisure
Down to fifteen-minute intervals

With no gods to guide us
We lost all sight of the never-ending
Birth, growth, death
And re-birth

Futile efforts to master nature
To stand apart from her

Only to be rebuked
By storms stripping strip malls
To their foundation

Though perhaps, entrusted
You and I to be her steward
Working with her
Never against
To share with her our vigilance
In gratitude for her gifts

To leave our campground
In better shape than we found it
To pull out the trash
Thrown into the lake

Or simply
Not to toss butts
Out the car window

You have said
Nature is sacred
And you have suspected
That worshiping her
Alone
At some indoor altar
Bedecked with spooky knickknacks
Is of far less use
Than picking up energy bar wrappers
Along a mountain trail

You have heard her call to you
While your spine malforms
To the cheapest office chair
Your boss could get away with
Sticking you in

Step outside the line
Step outside!

Wotan's Plea
by Carolyn Emerick

God of wisdom and of war,
gave us the runes and sired Thor.
His ravens o'er Midgard fly,
watching us from Asgard's skies.

Great warriors in death are called
to feast with him in his great hall.
The Folk worldwide, his sons and daughters
give respect to our Allfather.

But from his eye there falls a tear
for the fate that looms so near.
The warriors have lost their might,
his children have no will to fight.

The Folk have clearly lost their way,
and though the threat is clear as day,
our people hide their heads in sand,
lacking courage to take a stand.

Where are the genes we did inherit
from the mighty men of merit?
The blood of Vikings in my veins flows!
But in my kinfolk…I do not know.

Weakness and cowardice they portray.
Their own ancestors they now betray.

Perhaps they are in too much shock
to see that this is Ragnarok!

We must unite, and we must fight!
Or usher in our own twilight...
For our children's sake Wotan implores,
the Folk must stand, and we must roar!

The Valkyria
by Lennart Svensson

The valkyries talked about weapons and horses,
horses and weapons. And battle arrays,
adventures and treasures, scudding clouds,
surging waves and a deserted moor with a
lonely tree under a grey sky.

The valkyria is no more and the age of war
is about to end—but the valkyria mindset
lives on as a paragon for women
living "action as being"—for women
seeking rest in action, women
conducting operations to gain knowledge,
movement as a state of mind,
action raising you mentally.

The valkyria is gone but her mindset lives on.

The Roots of Trees
by Eirik Westcoat

Consider a tree, seemingly ordinary,
to learn the model and life of the others:
the tree within and the Tree without.
Of trees we see the trunk and branches
with beautiful leaves and bright flowers:
luscious wonders. But lurking beneath
the soil's surface are the secret roots
in that darkest realm of deep unknowns,
where mysteries lurk, tremendous Runes.
So, to truly know a tree's full life,
look to those roots and what lurks among them.
Look to your tree, and learn your mysteries.
Look to the Tree, and learn its Mysteries.
This initiation of needful growth
begins in darkness but goes to the light.
What will you find in your wondrous tree?
What will you find in the wondrous Tree?
Travel the trunk and take to the roots
for the worlds below and the wells with orlog.
Traditions slumber and dreams await,
deep in those roots. Dare to raise them,
lift what reposes from the Land of the Dead.
Find What was Lost, for its fimbul might
brings life anew to leaf and flower
on a tree that's troubled and triumph aplenty

to a tree that's strong. The truest of changes
are wrought with the boons from that realm below
which lead to the realm of light above,
the crown in the heights with its clear pure view.

Glorious
by Juleigh Howard-Hobson

So autumn ends. Vines wither to the ground,
Brown leaves fall in heaping drifts and cover
The land that soon shall fall asleep. Winds come
Bringing a bitter sting, borne of ice. Sound
Carries further in the cold, the other
World will reach out. Murmurs and whispers from
The frozen shadows, low hints of song that
Float soft on the frigid air: winter's breath
Blowing down your back. Clouds, heavy and hung
With darkened hints of storm, come. Grey and flat
Across a sky made all the heavier with
Winter's pull. Gloriously, down among
The rocks, along the cracks, underneath wings,
Life waits, in root, in nest, inside, for spring.

Argos
by David Yorkshire

And as I walk towards the garden gate,
My old companion totters up the drive
And I am older now and you are old
And we are in another time and place
And I remember back when you were bold
And hunted fallow deer and the wild boar
That turned when cornered, rounded savagely
And charged and fought, but were no match for you.

You do not see me through cataract eyes,
But then you stop and sniff the autumn air
And find my scent there floating on the breeze;
Your nose twitches excitedly, your snout,
Then body, tail are set in motion seized
With raw emotion and you come to me
As faithful now as when I must depart,
With old and creaking bones stretch gingerly
Up to my chest and slowly I reach down
With care and lift you up so you can see
My face again and see me one last time.

You who kept watch while I was far away,
Your time has come now: the last gleam of joy
That lights your eye no small reward to you
Whose duty now fulfilled may rest, but I,
Though tired, must fight the battle prophesied

And rescue this enslaved once fertile land
Now barren made with deconstructive ways
That are not ours, but made by foreign hands
That wander where they are not meant to pry—
In wallets, shorts and bodices are found
Molesting women, kids and bank accounts.

But now I think of these grave things no more,
For with a whimper half of wild despair
Yet half of joy that our two kindred hearts
May beat again together side by side
If but for one brief moment just before
One stops, the other left alone and starts
To compensate, beats twice as fast to hide
The loss, your final breath is lost to air,
And I lay you, a mere bundle of fur,
Upon the garden's sandy ground, my ear
Filled with the wind and distant sound of waves,
There to remind me that my epic tale
Began so long ago on other shores
In other times is not yet at an end.
So rest my weary watcher, rest you well,
While I must punish traitors hard and mend
A broken land, rid it of foreign thieves.

The King has returned, both hero and poet,
And my unwitting enemies shall know it
Soon, and this tale shall finish similar
To one told long ago and far away,
Yet not the same, no not the same for you;

For Homer learned a classic soul, but I
A born romantic, I adventurer,
I who rest a firm hand upon your head,
I give you the end that you should have had.

Sea of Stars
by Amelia Beechwood

If you listen closely your tinnitus may be
in actual fact:
The sounds of frogs and crickets singing
on those childhood night walks
in the country where the light is pitch,
the twinkling stars above brightly close;
and to your sides,
the woods full of blinking fireflies.
This, all surrounding you in a pulsing darkness that was
in actual fact:
A first taste of understanding.

We are floating in infinity.

By the Shores of My Mothers
by Albie A. Gogel

And by the shores of my Mothers did my mind roam...
Simple were the days,
yet nights kissed with the Magic of the Sea...
I learned much in this Tide of Moon,
from the Whisper of the Trees...
From the Mountains I drank of Purity,
my body tempered by the Ancient Seas...

Homecoming
by Jason O'Toole

In this estuary of the river
That flows both ways
Seahorse hunts on his lands
Tail curled around a ribbon
Of eelgrass

Cloaked in this sunken forest
Eyes search his quarry
A clutch of fish eggs
Seahorse strikes fast
Drawing them in
Through stubby snout

Under a crumbling pier
Where Mahicantuck opens to the sea
In the shallows where sunrays
Pierce the turbid waters
Seahorse anchors himself
To the seabed

Courage outlasting
The fate of wild past
Reeling back victorious
From annihilation's static border
Seahorse scans the poisoned waters

Brimming with creatures
Nature has made immune

Seahorse stalks ghost shrimp
To feed the many young
Growing in his pouch
Through the strength of his resolve
His tribe thrives
Restored to ancestral lands

Sumbel

by Christina Finlayson Taylor

Another moot we meet, and often in
Another place, and always *us*, plus more…
A swell of souls, partitions thin
To nil between us…here we hone the core
And grow organically a ring of trust;
Take measure, weaving parallel our ways;
And, fly or climb, the only way for us
Is up and forward, thrusting through the veins,

Yet always "here" at home. There's Love in here,
And Light. We love the darkness too. We do,
Create and shape—direction clear
Without defining words, and always true
To essence. We are One, the Wolf, the Tribe,
The thriving Tree of Life, eternal Ice,
Undying Flame with *Spirit* so alive,
It only grows. We will it *never die*.

Stonehenge
by Matthew Wildermuth

What mouth-less idiom here throbs the indurated
Heft of engulfed ages?—Enshadowed fathers,
To out-moan the wind as through your pillared clefts
It casts such chill, what could those now who yet
May thrill in the chant of your stern revenant
Invoke to reply through this impassable
Abysm through which you loom? We who suffer
Our fatal truth and mourn, and must mourn ever
The catastrophe of its depleting
Survey of all our hearts need most.

                As beyond
Your fate-fractured stonework, clasped so in frost,
An amaranthine flood, like of a dream,
Through the fading of the stars, heaves to wake again
—speak!

Nordic Sphinx
by Lennart Svensson

I'm a Nordic Sphinx,
looking out over the boundless hills,
seeing a bright future

for all and sundry—a future perfect,
an archaic future, a future in
purple and gold, silver and green.

The pine is ever green,
the sun casting its gold
on the mountain side,

the moon etching its silver runes
and the purple twilight—
the colors of a new era.

◆ ◆ ◆

I'm the king of comedy,
a metal guru and an
implicit whiteness.

I'm a prophet, a poet,
a preacher, a piper,
a guru, a sphinx,

an attic fanatic and a forest creature,
an aristocrat of the soul.

I'm a poet and a piper,
a prophet of Northernness
singing for the trees,

singing for the people,
singing for fun in an age
where no one seems to

be laughing any more, no one
smiles, no one feels the joy of anything.
There I come with my flute

throwing green melodies over
everyone, saying "life can be
fun too, you know."

◆ ◆ ◆

The prophet has spoken,
the guru is gone, the
Northern Sphinx has left

the building, left us for
the boundless hills, the
thousand-mile forest,

the moors and the swamps,
the grey-green expanses of
coniferous woods

holding a future for us all,
an old future, an archaic future:
archeo-future, a future perfect.

Sonne

by Juleigh Howard-Hobson

And it will come, our dawning, do not doubt…
Right now it doesn't seem like much, but we
Can already look and see the dark route
Ahead is lit a little. It was the
Bleakest path to take when we began. But,
We believed night couldn't last, believed our
Day would dawn, believed our steps would be put
In step with others—so they shall. Power
Of vision, of faith, of will, brings our sun;
With power to make manifest a sky
Gone bright with morning, gone bright with the one
Light that cannot be dimmed again. Our eyes
Are trained ahead, we'll watch the growing dawn
Illuminate our pathway. We'll push on.

The Thunderer's Might
by Albie A. Gogel

Mighty Thunar, scourge of Jötunheimr, brother of man...
Let the Thunderer walk within length of arm always...
Foremost of honor, father of the tribes,
central throne'd in Gamla Hall...
Mighty Mjölnir, crusher of þursar, splitter of skulls...
Sigil of power, symbol of might, gift of strength & precision...
Cyclical key of kinetic force, Sindri and Brokkr fame...
In Grjöttungard, where mighty ones charge, fell Mokkerkalfe,
where Ukko's hammer made Hrungnir's shard,
that stone pyramid once a heart...
Master of the Winds, Ol' Red's eyes,
those gateways of Mystery and akin to Dvalinn
gave Runa of Time,
Vitki taught from Fire of Eye, Fire of Mind...
Energies' Smith, that which animates, forms and unites,
radiating power that flows through all, Jörð's charge...
Protector of the Folk,
giver of fertility and virile fame,
cleanser of soil & souls...
In time of need, in time of strife, in Time...
Through Will of Old & Highest of SELF,
we share Thor's might...
That coursing strength, that lightning's strike,
within us we charged, released without...
Let our own belt of strength, our Megingjörð,

be Draupnir's kin & increase 9-fold...
Unto you, slayer of Þrymr,
wader of the torrent of swords...
Let our hammers always strike true...
May our Megingjörð be increased 9-fold...
Unto you, slayer of Þrymr,
wader of rivers all,
as we grip with Járngreipr our Mjölnir...
Like you, Father of Might,
let our hammers always strike true!

Calling the Tribe Homeward
by Carolyn Emerick

Behold, the Lady doth call out
with a voice clear and true,
to the Folk with the ears to hear,
she calleth out to you.

Hark! And hear the pipes do ring
like crystal through the ether.
We had been blind and lost before,
but now our Folk do gather.

Hear the call and heed the voice
that rallies for our kin.
The battle ahead will be intense,
but together, we will win!

Notes

[1] Siegfried Manteuffel's "Aurora" cycle was inspired by the birth of his child a few years ago. The intention was to provide some kind of guidance according to the spiritual aspects of his weltanschauung, as a blessing of the new life.

[2] Amelia Beechwood's note on ancient European spirituality (addenda to "In defense of Animism"): "When a tree comes to be viewed, no longer as the body of the tree-spirit, but simply as its abode which it can quit at pleasure, an important *advance* has been made in religious thought. Animism is passing into polytheism. In other words, instead of regarding each tree as a living and conscious being, man now sees in it merely a lifeless, inert mass, tenanted for a longer or shorter time by a supernatural being who, as he can pass freely from tree to tree, thereby enjoys a certain right of possession or lordship over the trees, and, ceasing to be a tree-soul, becomes a forest god. As soon as the tree-spirit is thus in a measure disengaged from each particular tree, he begins to change his shape and assume the body of a man, in virtue of a general tendency of early thought to clothe all abstract spiritual beings in concrete human forms."
  —Sir James Frazer *The Golden Bough.* Abridged Ed. (Mineola, NY: Dover Publications, 2002), p. 117.
**Author challenges the term "advance."

[3] Stuart Sudekum's note: "The poems within 'An Earthly Crown' comprise what is termed a 'crown of sonnets,' that is, fourteen poems of fourteen lines each, interwoven by using the last line of one as the first line of the next. These are bound together by a 'master sonnet,' which is composed of the first line of each of these. Tom Priestly has eloquently explicated the demanding formal considerations that must be made to achieve this in the commentary he produced on his translation of France Prešeren's *Wreath of Sonnets*. His explanation of the complicated rhyme scheme has been indispensable in my own attempt at it.

"In Prešeren's *Wreath*, he added the additional aspect of an acrostic to his master sonnet. I have followed his example in this regard, despite the fact that it creates some metrical difficulty.

"In my subject matter, I owe everything to Arthur Edward Waite, whose rich language of symbols has been for years the animating genius behind my own attempts to express something beyond the mundane existence of modern life. Where I have employed words that have passed mostly out of modern usage, I have restricted myself to language characteristic of northern England and Scotland, the geography of which region has inspired the setting of my narrative. Where poetic contraction appears, I have attempted to keep it infrequent and relied on accepted conventions of English poetry found in Edmund Spencer, etc. The alliterative aspects are influenced by old Scandinavian conventions and are intended to heighten the medieval tone by capturing something of the agile wordsmithing of the skalds."

[4] In "The Wise Elders," Christina's primary outer sources of runic understanding are Freya Aswynn's *Leaves of Yggdrasil* and Collin Cleary's "Philosophical Notes on the Runes." Furthermore, the idea leans heavily on a poem by the grandfather of artist Heidi Holder in her illustrated book *Crows: An Old Rhyme*; and on the feel of its delivery on Horse Cult's *Day Dreams & Night Mares* CD.

Acknowledgments

Amelia Beechwood:

"Voyage Within": lyrics for a song by Withering of Light (Todd Janeczek), sung by Amie Beckwith of Horse Cult <www.witheringoflight.bandcamp.com>.

Juleigh Howard-Hobson:

"Sonne" was first published in *Cycle of Nine* (RavensHalla, 2013).
"Sonnet to Freya" first appeared in *Eternal Haunted Summer* (2018).

Siegfried Manteuffel:

"The Axis" (English version) was published on *Aeon* (spring equinox, 2017) <http://erntegang.bandcamp.com/album/aeon-windzeit-wolfszeit>.
All other poems by Siegfried were published on *Aurora* (winter solstice, 2018) <http://erntegang.bandcamp.com/album/aurora>.

Jason O'Toole:

"Spring into Being" was first published in *Spear of Stars* (The Red Salon, 2018).

Lennart Svensson:

"Palearctic Grandeur," "The Glory of Hyboria," "The Valkyria" and "Vittra" first appeared in *Heathen Call* (Issue 9, Midsommar 2016).

Eirik Westcoat:

"Fólksdrápa" was first published in Eirik's *Viking Poetry for Heathen Rites* (2017).
"Hanging from a Tree" first appeared at <www.theskaldiceagle.com>.
"Óðinsdrápa" was first published in Eirik's *Eagle's Mead* (2019).
"Rise and Reach the Gods" was first published in Eirik's *Viking Poetry for Heathen Rites* (2017).
"The Roots of Trees" first appeared at <www.theskaldiceagle.com>.

Troy Wisehart:

"Lords of the Black Flame," "That of Which I Am" and "The Tasks of the Ages" were previously published in *Ethereal Darkness* (2017).

Biographies

Amelia Beechwood has many simultaneous incarnations. She writes lyrics for and performs with Horse Cult and other musical projects as Amie Beckwith; curates and organizes seasonal and esoteric art events as Virgo Moon; creates installations of the temporal-sacred as Zeitliches Sakral; and once upon a time hosted works by others (some found within these pages) as A. von Rautmann. She currently resides in Portland, Oregon with her family, practicing bodywork and longing for the countryside.

Carolyn Emerick researches and writes about Northern European cultural mytho-history and ethno-spiritualism. See her work at www.CarolynEmerick.com.

Albie A. Gogel grew up around the New Jersey coastline and now resides amid the mountains and swirling leaves of Northeast Pennsylvania. He is a longtime student of comparative mythology and religion with focus on Old Norse studies, Germanic and Celtic streams of Indo-European pre-Christian spirituality. He uses the same methodology in esoteric and occult studies. His poems have appeared in *Mimir: Journal of North European Traditions* and *Vor Tru Magazine*.

Juleigh Howard-Hobson writes numinous poetry. She has been nominated for "The Best of the Net," The Pushcart Prize and a Rhysling. Her latest book is *Our Otherworld* (The Red Salon). She lives in the cold grey wilds of the Pacific Northwest USA where she practices useful Northern magic.

Siegfried Manteuffel was born in 1976 in Germany. Having a deeper interest in the occult underground and spiritual counter currents since the early 1990s, he has been active with some small projects in the underground music scene since the mid-90s. He studied at Braunschweig University, works as a civil engineer, and is a father of one daughter. He has run the music project Erntegang (bearing spiritual/pagan overtones) since 2007 and currently resides in Lower Saxony, Germany.

Jason O'Toole is the author of *Spear of Stars* (The Red Salon, 2018) and was featured in *An Anthology of Poems from The Red Salon* (2018). His writing has appeared in *Heathen Harvest Periodical*, *Nixes Mate Review*, *Tigershark* and countless fanzines and one-shots. He was the vocalist for NY Hardcore Punk band, Life's Blood. He performs spoken word backed by musician and composer, Alec K. Redfearn.

Stuart Sudekum is a writer and educator on the subject of European religious history and culture. He has lectured on the western esoteric tradition for a number of organizations and institutions, including the New York School of Visual Arts (SVA), Morbid Anatomy Museum, and the Seattle Esoteric Book Conference. His writing has appeared in periodicals such as *Clavis Journal* and *Heathen Harvest*, and he provides guitar and vocals for Apibus, an experimental folk music ensemble.

Lennart Svensson (1965-) is a Swede both writing in Swedish and English. In the latter language, he has for instance published the novels *Burning Magnesium* (2018) and *Redeeming Lucifer* (2017), and the essays *Actionism* (2017), *Borderline* (2015) and *Science Fiction Seen from the Right* (2016).

Christina Finlayson Taylor manages two publishing imprints (Middle Island Press and The Red Salon) and is the author of three books of poetry and verse: *Villanelles & Varia* (2010), *Near-Life Experience* (2018) and *The Colors of My Soul* (2018). She resides in West Virginia with her husband and their son.

Eirik Westcoat is a long-time Asatruar who has presented his award-winning poetry at several regional Asatru gatherings in the American Northeast. He writes mainly in Old Norse and Old English poetic meters. He has published two books so far: *Viking Poetry for Heathen Rites* (2017), a book of Asatru religious poetry, and the recently-released *Eagle's Mead* (2019), a book of esoteric initiatory poetry and prose. He is a member of the Rune-Gild, and that latter book presents a rare poetic look at the process of runic initiation. He also has written articles on the Old Norse *galdralag* poetic meter and the meaning of the valknut.

Matthew Wildermuth is a father, poet, and video artist living near the banks of the Missouri in North Dakota. His work has appeared and is forthcoming in various literary journals, including *The Society of Classical Poets*, *Terror House*, and *Concentric Literary Magazine*. His first collection of original verse, *The Ruin*, is forthcoming through The Red Salon.

Troy Wisehart is the author of *Ethereal Darkness*, a collection of twenty-four poems about Norse mythology and magic. Troy also has a recording and live performance music project called Wodhanazson. He lives in Seattle, Washington with his wife and is active in Heathenry as well as Freemasonry. *Ethereal Darkness* and Wodhanazson recordings are available on Amazon. Troy can be contacted via his Facebook page.

David Yorkshire was educated in several European countries and is the editor of *Mjolnir Magazine*, both a print magazine for the Eurocentric illiberal creative arts and an online blog. He also co-hosts "Mjolnir at the Movies," a regular podcast reviewing films and their influence on popular culture. He writes short stories, plays and poetry and contributes articles to various publications and edited the English translation of Hans-Jürgen Syberberg's *On the Misfortune and Fortune of Art in Post-War Germany*.

Made in the
USA
Monee, IL